# ELEPHANTS

A N I M A L    F A M I L I E S

# ELEPHANTS

Annette Barkhausen and Franz Geiser

Gareth Stevens Publishing
**MILWAUKEE**

**For a free color catalog describing Gareth Stevens's list of high-quality books, call 1-800-341-3569 (USA) or 1-800-461-9120 (Canada).**

The editor would like to extend special thanks to Elizabeth S. Frank, Curator of Large Mammals at the Milwaukee County Zoo, Milwaukee, Wisconsin, for her kind and professional help with the information in this book.

At this time, Gareth Stevens, Inc., does not use 100 percent recycled paper, although the paper used in our books does contain about 30 percent recycled fiber. This decision was made after a careful study of current recycling procedures revealed their dubious environmental benefits. We will continue to explore recycling options.

*Below: A 3,000-year-old bronze elephant figure from the Chinese province of Shaanxi.*

**Library of Congress Cataloging-in-Publication Data**

Barkhausen, Annette.
   [Elefanten. English]
   Elephants / by Annette Barkhausen and Franz Geiser.
     p. cm. — (Animal families)
   Includes bibliographical references (p. ) and index.
   Summary: a discussion of elephants, their history, description, behavior, and language, with details on the differences between African and Asian elephants.
   ISBN 0-8368-1001-5
   1. Elephants—Juvenile literature. [1. Elephants.] I. Geiser, Franz. II. Title.
   III. Series: Animal families (Milwaukee, Wis.)
   QL737.P98B2613 1993
   599.6'1—dc20                                        93-13049

North American edition first published in 1994 by
**Gareth Stevens Publishing**
1555 North RiverCenter Drive, Suite 201
Milwaukee, Wisconsin 53212, USA

This edition first published in 1994 by Gareth Stevens, Inc. Original edition © 1992 by Kinderbuchverlag KBV Luzern AG, Lucerne, Switzerland, under the title *Elefanten.* Adapted by Gareth Stevens, Inc. All additional material supplied for this edition © 1994 by Gareth Stevens, Inc.

Series editor: Patricia Lantier-Sampon
Editor: Barbara J. Behm
Translated from the German by Jamie Daniel
Editorial assistants: Diane Laska and Andrea Schneider
Editorial consultant: Elizabeth S. Frank

Printed in Mexico

1 2 3 4 5 6 7 8 9 9 99 98 97 96 95 94

*Right: An African elephant cow with her calf.*

# Table of Contents

# What Is an Elephant?

We have all grown up with certain ideas of what elephants are like. As children, we first saw images of elephants in picture books and in cartoons. We became accustomed to the appearance of this fascinating, trunked animal and enchanted by its behaviors.

Elephants have uncommonly long, mobile trunks. The main purpose of the trunk is to transfer food and water to the animal's mouth. But the trunk also provides the elephant with a way to taste, touch, and smell. This is important, since an elephant's sense of sight, though keen, is often restricted because of the animal's size.

The trunk is both sensitive and strong at the same time. With its trunk, an elephant can pick up a small twig as well as an enormous log. Fine hairs located at the tip of the trunk can detect scents from afar. Physical touch with one another is very important to elephants. Physical contact between mother and child is very important. This contact is maintained with the trunk.

The elephant's tusks are sometimes as long as 3 feet (1 meter), and its ears are huge and floppy. Elephant skin is marked with ridges and creases, especially on the trunk and forehead.

Elephants are constantly on the move, traveling to areas within their territory where water and food are available. They also move about in search of shade and a place to rest.

Elephants associate with one another harmoniously as families. Each family unit contains closely related females, or cows, and their young, called *calves*. Adult males only occasionally visit the family unit for the sole purpose of mating.

The elephants in each family are very affectionate and gentle with one another. They respect each other's position in the family hierarchy. When an elephant greets another family member who has a higher rank, the lower animal may thrust the tip of its trunk into the mouth of the higher ranking animal as a sign of submission. Animals in each group make throaty, rumbling sounds as they move about, taking part in their daily routine. The constant rumbling noise is the means by which family members keep in close communication with one another.

A family contains about twelve members, on average. Sometimes, many different family units will come together in a large herd for a time, but they will eventually break up again into the smaller units.

A mature female member of each family unit is the matriarch, or leader, of the unit. Usually, the family consists of her descendants. Each member of the group greatly respects the matriarch because of her wisdom, age, and experience. Family members rely on her guidance and judgement. When a matriarch dies, the next eldest female assumes the role.

Although the elephant is extremely large and powerful, it is a peaceful animal. An adult elephant in modern times basically has no other predators to fear except humans. People have hunted the mighty elephant for the past twenty thousand years. Humans hold within their grasp the power either to

Far left: An elephant coin from 281 B.C. Center: A coin from the time of Caesar showing an elephant treading on a snake. Immediate left: A silver coin from 48 B.C.

Below: The elephant-headed deity Ganesha, the god of wisdom, is located in a temple in India. The deity rides atop a rat, and its belly is so fat because it is supposed to contain all of nature.

*Right: This Roman mosaic shows an African elephant. The people of ancient Rome used elephants in battle.*

*Below: Hannibal's war elephants in a battle with Roman foot soldiers. The elephants looked intimidating, but they were easily overcome because they were exhausted by the long march into battle.*

protect the elephant for all to enjoy in the future or to destroy the animal completely.

### Of Elephants and Humans

Humans and elephants must have encountered one another early on in the course of history. There would have been no way for them to overlook each other! But people in Africa behaved differently toward the giant animals than did the people in Asia.

In Africa, people hunted elephants and trained them for different tasks. In Asia, on the other hand, people honored the elephant. In India, for example, people were so in awe of the elephant's strength and size that they worshipped several elephant deities. The most famous of these is the elephant deity Ganesha. It is considered the destroyer of all impediments and the god of wisdom. For these reasons, it is the patron god of writers.

*Right:  A beautifully carved elephant chess figure.  It comes from southern Italy and was carved toward the end of the eleventh century.*

*Below, right:  The giant circus elephant Jumbo was very popular during the nineteenth century.*

The elephant's big ears are said to be of help in selecting the honest or genuine words from the language of humans.   The second important elephant deity in India is Airavata, the animal ridden by the god Indra.   In addition, there are a multitude of other elephant deities in India, Sri Lanka, China, and Indonesia.

In early times, people in Asia also made use of the enormous strength and powerful appearance of the trunked animal. Elephants worked as laborers.  Indian lords kept hundreds of elephants for use in battle. During peacetime, columns of expensively decorated parade elephants marched in large celebrations.   This increased the status of their owner.

The Carthaginian general Hannibal marched against Rome in the year 218 B.C. with thirty-seven African battle elephants. On the long journey across Spain, southern France, and the Alps, however, many of the elephants lost their lives. Those that survived lost their strength and were too weak to help Hannibal win the battle, and he was soundly defeated by the Romans.

An elephant named Abbul Abbas was the first elephant brought to northern Central Europe.  He was a gift from a southern lord in honor of the coronation of Charlemagne in the year 800.   Much later, in the sixteenth century, Kaiser Maximillian had an elephant brought to Vienna, Austria.  Both of these animals were forced to walk the enormous distance from the Mediterranean to their new homes.  They both died within a few years of their arrival due to the cold and damp weather of Europe.  Only later did people realize that,

like all animals, elephants have special needs that must be met if they are to survive.

The most famous elephant in Europe during the nineteenth century was an extraordinarily large elephant named Jumbo. He made his home in the London Zoo.  Even today, especially large objects are named after him.  For example, think of the packaging on products in the grocery store that advertises a "jumbo" size or the giant airplane known as a "jumbo jet."  The real Jumbo was a celebrity

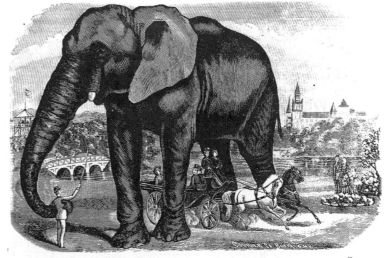

**This is how the elephant's body evolved (from bottom illustration to top) in the course of millions of years.**

**The** Moeritherium **could have looked like the little animal at the bottom forty million years ago. The three other illustrations represent**

**different evolutionary forms of mastodons with increasingly long tusks and trunks.**

in Britain for years. He was later transferred to the United States and was just as popular there. When Jumbo died in 1885, the entire world mourned his passing.

### Prehistoric Elephants and Mammoth Bones

Humans and elephants share a long history together, but there were elephantlike animals on Earth long before there were people. Today's elephants are the remaining members of a race of trunked animals that once lived almost everywhere in the world. These animals originated in prehistoric times. Scientists estimate that the earliest predecessors of elephants evolved about fifty million years ago from the ancestors of rock hyrax and manatees. Little rock hyraxes, which are only the size of woodchucks, and the giant manatees that live in the ocean are the nearest living relatives of today's elephants.

The remains of an animal about 28 inches (70 centimeters) in length were found along the Moeris Lake in Egypt. Scientists called the animal *Moeritherium*, which means "Moeris-animal." It lived about forty million years ago in a wet, swampy area near the lake. Even now, researchers disagree as to whether it was a predecessor of elephants or of manatees. It did not have a trunk or tusks.

Other animals called *mastodons*, which are now extinct, looked much more like elephants. These giant animals originated in Africa. They extended as far as Europe, Asia, and the Americas about twenty million years ago. They were a large group of animals that included many species. Early mastodons

**Left:** *The mammoth's thick hair protected it from the cold in its Ice Age habitat. Mammoths disappeared when the Ice Age ended about ten thousand years ago.*

**Below:** *It is hard to believe that the rock hyrax is one of the elephant's closest relatives. Both animals evolved from the same ancestors.*

had a short trunk and tusks that grew from the upper and lower jaw. The later mastodons, that died out about ten thousand years ago, looked very similar to today's elephants.

The mammoth is the most widely recognized elephant relative. Now extinct, mammoths lived in Europe and Asia during the Ice Age. They ate grass just like today's elephants. They reached heights of 11 feet (3.4 m) and more — and were thus at least as large as today's African elephants. With their thick coats of hair, they were well-adapted to the cold climate of the time. Their tusks, which were sharply curved and up to 16.5 feet (5 m) long, must have been an incredible sight. Many scientists believe mammoths used their giant teeth to clear away snow and

to test the ground to see whether it was secure enough to walk on. There were many bottomless swamps in the cold habitat of the mammoths, and sometimes the swamps were covered by a layer of ice. Animals often fell through the ice and were trapped inside the depths of the swamps. These swamps, in fact, are the places where animal fossils are most often discovered. Bones of Ice Age woolly rhinos, wild horses, bison, wolves, and mammoths have all been found at these sites.

Scientists are not sure why mammoths died out when the Ice Age ended about ten thousand years ago. Perhaps they were not able to adapt to the warmer climate. But it is also possible that Stone Age hunters had something to do with the animals' disappearance. People of that time hunted the mammoth for its meat, its hide, and its bones. In the Ukraine and Russia, human settlements have been found that are fifteen thousand years old. The ancient structures located there are built almost entirely of mammoth bones. For example, about one hundred mammoth skulls were used to build a single round bone hut about 16.5 feet (5 m) in diameter.

Today, Siberia's constantly frozen tundra still contains well-preserved mammoth bodies. In 1799, a frozen mammoth was

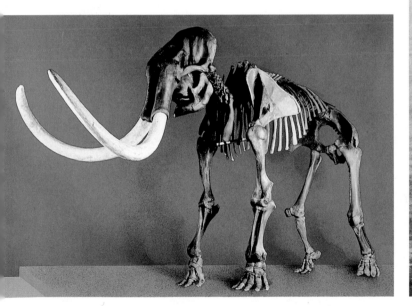

found in the muddy delta at the mouth of the Lena River that was beginning to thaw out. The animal still had all its flesh, skin, and hair. Scientists in St. Petersburg did not hear about the discovery until seven years later but were at least able to save the skeleton. When the scientists examined the skeleton, they discovered that the tusks had been hacked off. Because the scientists had no way of knowing any differently, they positioned the tusks incorrectly, with the tips pointed

outward. The skeleton was taken back to St. Petersburg and served as a model, or prototype, for many other museums. Thus, mammoth skeletons were reconstructed throughout Europe at that time with the tusks pointing in the wrong direction. This error was discovered only in the last several decades.

### Tools for Survival

The major identifying feature of the elephant is its trunk. The trunk consists of a long,

*Opposite: An elephant in Zimbabwe eats from a tree. The elephant is able to pull down tender branches with its trunk from a height of about 20 feet (6 m).*

*Right: An elephant drinks by spraying water into its mouth. The wet spots on its cheeks have been caused by secretions from its temple glands.*

extended nose with an upper lip. About forty thousand muscles running longitudinally and diagonally account for the remarkable degree of mobility in the trunk.

With this strong, agile trunk, the elephant can tear trees out of the ground as well as accomplish detailed work, such as picking

*Right: The end of the African elephant's long trunk is equipped with two grasping, fingerlike extensions.*

*Far right: The Asian elephant has only one gripping finger.*

up a coin from the ground. The extremely sensitive trunk of the African elephant has two fingerlike extensions, or gripping fingers, while the Asian elephant has just one. Both types of elephants are capable of precise tasks, such as picking up a stick with the tip of the trunk and using it to scratch its body.

With its trunk, an elephant can reach food as far away as 20 feet (6 m) and put it in its mouth. With its trunk, an elephant can also take in 2.5 gallons (9.5 liters) of water at a time and spray them into its mouth. An elephant also blows dust out of its trunk onto

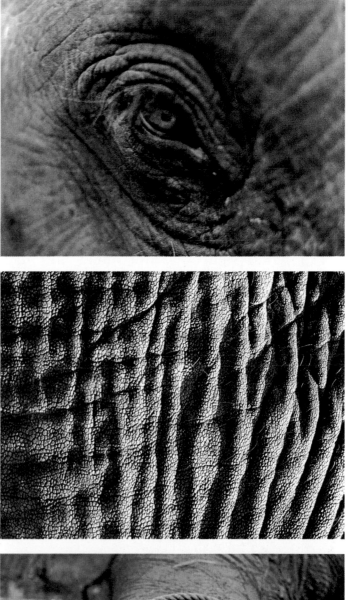

its body as protection from insects and other parasites. And the elephant breathes through its trunk. When crossing a deep river, it can use its upheld trunk as a snorkel.  It can breathe through the trunk even if the rest of its body is completely underwater.

Elephants make a loud trumpeting noise with their trunks when excited or agitated. Some Asian elephants have even learned to whistle through their trunks. Elephants also have an excellent sense of smell.  They use their trunks to pick up scents of friends or foes or to locate a distant watering hole.

The second key identifying characteristic of the elephant is its tusks.  Both male (bulls) and female (cows) African elephants have tusks.    However, only *some* of the Asian elephants have tusks, and these are *all* bulls.

The largest African elephant tusks on record are 10 feet (3 m) long and together weigh 440 pounds (200 kg). Today, however,

most elephants' tusks do not reach this size. Although the sale and trade of ivory is forbidden in many countries, tusks are still bought and sold by the ton, especially in the Far East.

Elephants use their tusks to dig up the earth when nearby water holes are dry. Elephants also use their tusks to mine for salty mineral deposits to supplement their diets, to peel bark off trees, to scare away rivals, and to make an impression on the opposite sex. But the elephant's tusks are not essential to its survival. Elephants whose tusks are removed to save them from poachers seem to get along just as well as they did with their tusks.

However, the molar teeth with which elephants grind their food are absolutely essential. Each molar is about the size of a brick and is covered with a hard enamel for chewing grass, rinds, and wood. The upper and lower jaw is equipped with six molars in each half jaw, for a total of twenty-four. But only one of these is used at a time. As a tooth is used up, it moves forward and is expelled at the front of the jaw. At the same time, the

**Left: A baby elephant nurses on milk from its mother.**

**Below: The lower jaw of an elephant with the brick-sized molars on both sides. As one molar is used up, it is pushed forward by new ones.**

the elephant's head is its trunk. The trunk's powerful muscles need a sufficient support system across the skull.

A large part of the elephant's brain is used to control its powerful body muscles. But the rest is used for astonishing feats of memory and intelligence. Asian elephant trainers know these elephants can recognize particular people after years or even decades have passed. In one test, a young female elephant was able to differentiate forty different pictures and memorize them. She was still able to

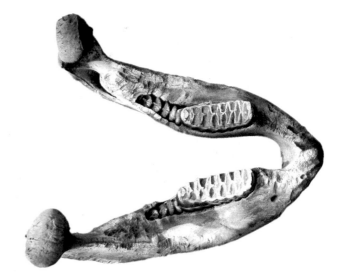

next tooth will push forward into the chewing zone. An elephant's set of teeth usually lasts about sixty-five years.

### The Elephant's Head

The elephant's large head is very impressive. Many people wonder what the elephant might be thinking behind such a mighty brow. Although elephants are very intelligent animals, their large skulls contain mostly air. A massive head with an equally massive brain would be much too heavy and impossible to support. An elephant's head, therefore, contains numerous air-filled pockets. Its brain, at about 12 pounds (5.5 kg), is more than three times as heavy as a human brain. But in comparison to the elephant's huge head size, its brain is relatively small.

You may wonder why elephants have such big skulls if they are mostly filled with air. The tusks are partly responsible for this, since they need a heavy skull to be securely anchored. But the main reason for the size of

repeat her performance a year later. Elephants also prove their intelligence through their behavior in the wild and the successful manner in which they raise their young.

An elephant's ears are also very important. Elephants have an acute sense of hearing. Giant ear flaps help elephants hear much better than humans and also serve as a means of cooling the animal. Because the

elephant's body is so big, cooling it down is difficult. Blood vessels covering the surface of the ears allow the animals to release excess heat into the air. Also, elephants do not have sweat glands, so they are unable to cool themselves off by perspiring. This cooling function explains why African elephants have

much bigger ears than their Asian cousins. African elephants live in hot, dry savannas; Asian elephants live more in shaded and wooded regions.

*Above: An elephant performs in a circus. In spite of their considerable weight, elephants can walk very precisely.*

*Left: Elephants are intelligent and learn how to perform very quickly.*

Female elephants can weigh up to four tons and males up to six or seven tons. This great weight is supported on four thick, column-shaped legs. Elephants' feet are equipped with thick "pillows" of ligature that cushion their step and elastically adapt to any surface. In spite of an elephant's great weight, it treads very softly and quietly upon the earth. An elephant's stable underframe, although it may appear to be awkward, can accomplish unbelievable acts of endurance. An elephant taking long strides can maintain a speed of from 7 to 9 miles (11 to 14 km) per hour for several hours. And, if in a hurry, an elephant can reach a short-distance speed of nearly 25 miles (40 km) per hour. The only thing an elephant cannot do, in spite of its light-footedness, is jump. This is why a moat 6.5 feet (2 m) deep and 6.5 feet (2 m) wide is sufficient to keep zoo elephants contained.

*Top: Elephant figurines made of a variety of materials.*

*Above: A herd of African elephants.*

*Right: Elephants are strong and fast, but they cannot jump — even over short distances.*

▲ *African elephant*

# A Guide to Elephants

▼ *Asian elephants*

# African Elephants

*Scientific name:* Loxodonta africana
*Height standing:* 8-13 feet (2.4-4 m)
*Weight:* cows, 4.5-5 tons
    bulls, up to 6 or 7 tons
*Life expectancy:* 50 to 65 years

An African elephant differs in many ways from an Asian elephant. For example, African elephants are generally somewhat larger. African elephant bulls and cows both have tusks, while only Asian elephant bulls have tusks. The tip of an African elephant trunk has two fingerlike extensions, or gripping fingers, while the Asian elephant trunk has only one. The African elephant has larger ears, a broader forehead, and a more saddle-shaped back than the Asian elephant.

Originally, African elephants lived across the entire continent of Africa. Today, they have disappeared from northern Africa and portions of southern Africa. They can mainly be found in the center region of the continent. And the elephants are still retreating. In the last ten years alone, Africa has lost more than half of its elephants. The elephants' natural habitat is being destroyed, and well-organized bands of poachers shoot the elephants for their valuable tusks.

## Plains Elephants and Forest Elephants

African elephants do not look the same in every region of the country. In eastern and southern Africa, elephants of the open plains and savannas are large and have giant ears that end in a point. Because they live on the plains where there is little shade, these elephants need big ears to help them keep cool. In western Africa, the elephants are forest dwellers. Because they live in shaded habitats, their ears are smaller and rounder on the bottom. These elephants also adapt to the thick forest by being smaller than the plains elephants and having straight tusks that point downward. Some people think these elephants make up a separate species, but they are all different varieties of the same species. In areas where the forest and the plains meet, the two types will often have mixed features.

**Above: Elephants spray dust on their backs as protection against sunburn and insect bites.**

**Opposite: In the Tsavo National Park in Kenya, a herd of African elephants makes a stop at a watering hole.**

## Marks on the Landscape

Whether they live on the plains or in the forest, elephants always need an open watering hole nearby. They drink between 18 to 26 gallons (70 to 100 liters) of water daily and also enjoy taking a full bath in muddy water. Depending on the color of the mud, the gray elephants can come out of the "tub" for about eighteen hours to satisfy their enormous nutritional requirements. Elephants need to eat between 330 and 375 pounds (150 and 170 kg) of grass, bark, and tree branches per day. When elephants are hungry, they don't curb their appetites for the sake of their environment. They simply uproot small and medium-sized trees in order to eat

a completely different color — from pale yellow to brown or even black.

Elephants are extremely poor at recognizing what would be good for them to eat, and they usually eliminate a great part of what they have eaten soon after eating. This means the elephants have to eat continuously the branches. They can damage giant baobab trees by peeling off bark and slashing the trees with their tusks until the trees die. In the eastern African national parks where many elephants are forced to live in too small a space, they can do serious damage to the area's trees.

In the past, elephants lived only in regions where there were natural watering holes and rivers. In such areas, the plant growth was so luxurious it could tolerate the elephants' grazing. But in recent decades, people have built watering holes in areas with only sparse plant growth. This water draws more elephants than the plant growth can feed.

Elephants also have a positive effect on their environment, however. Because they eat the fruits of trees and then later pass out the seeds in their waste, they indirectly plant new trees. Secondly, in rain forests the elephants' eating habits create small holes in the forest cover. This creates clearings for new animal and plant life. In the dry savannas, elephants dig watering holes from which other animals also can drink, including rhinoceroses and buffalo.

**Above: Young elephants in a family herd are protected by the older animals.**
**Below: Elephants also use their trunks for playing games and expressing affection.**

Above: Two elephant bulls fighting.
Below: Elephants enjoy bathing because the water supports their weight, and they are able to relax.

## A Friendly Family Herd

In the 1960s, Scottish researcher Iain Douglas-Hamilton became the first human to live among the African elephants. He observed and noted elephant behavior. Some years later, Cynthia Moss of the United States continued this research. She observed four families of elephants in the Amboseli National Park in Africa for thirteen years. She noted their daily and annual rituals, took part in their struggles to survive through periods of drought, and recorded their births and deaths. Because of this research, much is now known about the behaviors of African elephant herds.

African elephants live in family groups. Each family is usually made up of an old, experienced lead cow, her grown or half-grown daughters, and their offspring. Such groups usually have between five and twenty animals. Together with other families, they form a loosely related herd that can easily have as many as fifty or sixty members.

Elephant males leave their mother's herd when they reach puberty. The males then move around with each other in bull groups. Males might also go off on their own. Occasionally, bulls visit the female herds in order to mate with females. But they stay only a few days and then return to their former group. If several bulls compete for a single female, the strongest bull will win.

Now and then, there is a battle between two bulls over a female. When this happens, the two bulls stand across from each other head to head and attempt to push the other away. These battles are usually fought between young bulls who want to test their strength. Grown bulls rarely fight. This is because they usually have known each other since their youth and already have established who is the strongest. Serious fights in which a bull is wounded or killed are rare.

Life in the family herds of females and young animals is characterized by an atmosphere of affection and consideration. The herd members, who are all related to one another, form close relationships. They often rub affectionately against each other, lean their heads together, and put their trunks in each others' mouths as a sign of particular friendship. Fights or misunderstandings among members do not occur often. It is to

**Below: Elephants sometimes dig their own watering holes.**

the younger elephants' advantage to follow the lead cow because she has had far more experience than they. When danger threatens, she knows best what to do with her family. In periods of drought, she knows where to find marshes that still have water and food.

### The Elephants' Language

When a herd of elephants pushes through the thick forest, the animals are not able to see each other. But their excellent sense of smell keeps them near their family members. Even more important to their ability to stay together is a deep growling or rumbling sound the elephants produce in their larynx. In 1983, zoologist Judith Berg listed ten different expressive sounds made by African elephants that help them communicate with each other.

*Above: In swampy areas, elephants bathe and eat the vegetation. Below: On eastern Africa's Mount Elgon, elephants have dug salt out of stone for centuries.*

Several years ago, American researcher Katherine Payne realized elephants could call to each other across great distances through infrasonic sounds. Infrasonic sounds are so deep that humans can't hear them at all. Dr. Payne discovered these sounds one day when she was standing near a zoo elephant. As she stood there, she noticed vibrations in the air. She felt pressure waves, such as those that can sometimes be sensed when a storm approaches. She then used scientific instruments to confirm the existence of infrasonic communications. These super-deep sounds can be heard by elephants more than 7.5 miles (12 km) away.

**Above: Elephants drink from humanmade watering holes in Wankie National Park in Zimbabwe.**

**Below: In western Africa, such as the scene below in Nigeria, elephants are forest-dwellers.**

### An Elephant's Temper

Whenever a herd of elephants notices anything unusual in its surroundings, the elephants' constant grumbling and rumbling will momentarily come to a stop. The animals immediately sense that danger is present. Mothers call their calves to safety by flapping their ears against their heads. All the elephants will raise their trunks over their heads and test the air for scents carried by the wind. For a while, the herd stands silently in the dust, trying to discover the source of the danger.

But the atmosphere is different when elephants are seriously frightened or are under attack. Under those conditions, the air vibrates with the noise of many elephants trumpeting at once. The trumpeting is accompanied by the further sounds of the elephants banging their trunks against the ground. In addition, the elephants flap their ears outward and shake their heads back and forth. They do this in order to make themselves look bigger and more threatening to their enemies.

It is at such moments that a good lead cow will show why she has attained her rank. She, the oldest and most experienced animal in the herd, will be the first to confront the enemy, be it human or lion. The younger elephants will press together behind her for protection. When a giant elephant cow charges like this through a cloud of dust, the enemy will almost certainly be afraid!

Whether an elephant decides to attack in earnest or not usually depends on its previous experience. Most elephants react to people and their vehicles with more caution than anger. In the Manjara National Park in Africa, Iain Douglas-Hamilton knew four elephant cows that attacked his car and tossed it around like a toy. Douglas-Hamilton knew that he had done nothing to provoke the attack. Therefore, he concluded that these four elephants had already had bad experiences with people who lived on a neighboring farm. Once these particular elephants had these bad experiences, they couldn't forget them. They couldn't see humans as anything but the enemy.

### An Elephant's Life

Elephant young are born after a gestation period, or pregnancy, of twenty-two months. This is the longest gestation period in the animal kingdom. An elephant cow is first

**Below: Too many elephants are often forced to live in too small an area. When this happens, the animals can cause serious damage to trees while trying to find food.**

able to become pregnant when she is ten years old, but normally only becomes pregnant once every four years.

An elephant baby, or calf, weighs about 220 pounds (100 kg) and is 3 feet (1 m) long at birth. Immediately after the birth, the mother and aunts attend to the baby. Within a half hour of being born, the baby is sturdy enough to stand on its own feet between its mother's front legs to nurse. Although the baby can walk very soon after birth, however, it takes many months to fully control the hundreds of thousands of muscles in its trunk. The baby drinks about 2-1/2 gallons (9.5 l) of nourishing milk from its mother a day. It nurses for between two and three years but also begins to eat small amounts of solid food a few weeks after birth. The calf's tusks begin to show at about two years of age. It is at this time that the mother encourages the baby to stop nursing.

About a third of all elephants born do not survive their first year of life, and half of all those born do not live to adulthood. They fall victim to predators, die of illnesses, or die of starvation or thirst during periods of drought. But if a baby elephant does survive, it will soon grow into a spirited, energetic young elephant that reaches puberty when it is between eight and twelve years old. At that stage, young bulls are driven from the herd. Young cows, on the other hand, stay and help raise their younger siblings until the cows are old enough to have offspring of their own.

*Above: Impounded elephant tusks in Sudan.*

*Left: Poachers kill an elephant in Uganda.*

*Opposite: This was Ahmed, Africa's largest elephant. He was approximately 13 feet (4 m) tall and had tusks about 10 feet (3 m) long. He died of old age in 1976.*

# Asian Elephants

*Scientific name:* Elephas maximus
*Height standing:* 8-10 feet (2.5-3 m)
*Weight:* up to 4.5 tons
*Life expectancy: 30 to 40 years in the wild, up
to 69 years in captivity*

Asian elephants differ from African elephants in many ways: Asian elephants are somewhat smaller; only some of the bulls have visible tusks; the tip of the trunk ends in just one gripping finger; and they have smaller ears, an arched forehead, and a rounder back.

Asian elephants once inhabited a huge territory extending from the point where the Euphrates and Tigris rivers meet across southern Asia to the Yangtze River in China. Shortly before the beginning of the rainy season, the herds would move into the river valleys to wait for rain and the fresh shoots of young grass. There, they would drink their fill and bathe. The cows would bring their young into the world at this time, so the calves could begin their lives when the best food was readily available.

### Everything Revolves Around the Babies

Beginning many years ago, however, humans forced elephants out of the fruitful river valleys into a few relatively small wooded areas. But even today, calves are born there when living conditions are most favorable.

Raising an elephant baby is extremely time-consuming, and a mother elephant cannot do it alone. A grown elephant must spend sixteen to eighteen hours a day eating and must sleep for at least three hours. The remaining time isn't enough to nurture, feed, and clean a baby and watch over the baby when it naps, plays, and bathes. A mother elephant needs the help of the other females. A younger elephant cow will stand by so the baby has both a mother and an extra baby-

sitter to take care of it. In fact, the entire herd concerns itself with grooming, defending, and watching over a young calf. As previously stated, an elephant birth is fairly rare, so every surviving calf is treasured by the herd. A cow gives birth only once every four years. Females can get pregnant starting at about the age of eight. At ten years, each cow will

**Above: This young Asian elephant moves confidently through its lush natural environment.**

**Opposite: Work elephants in India carry tree trunks weighing several tons.**

have its first calf, which will be nursed for two years. Only when this calf has been weaned, or no longer drinking its mother's milk, will a cow be fertile again.

Swiss zoologist Fred Kurt discovered more methods used by elephants to make certain calves have a good start in life. Herds of mothers with babies are always allowed by

## When Bulls Become Dangerous

Sometimes a bull will secrete a black, oily, strong-smelling substance from glands in his temples. This signals a period of unpredictable behavior called *musth*. An elephant bull in musth will want to mate with a female and is extremely aggressive. In this condition, the bull is especially dangerous toward people.

other elephants to use the areas with the richest supply of food and water. Mothers with older calves move over to allow mothers with young calves to have the best food and water. Males of mating age are expected to use the least fertile areas. Males often travel long distances in search of new food supplies.

He will also defeat any bull that tries to fight with him, unless that bull is also "in musth."

In order to be in musth, a bull must be an adult of at least fifteen years of age. This means that he has already been sexually mature for about six years. A bull in musth will go to the herds that have babies, for it is there he will encounter mature cows that are fertile. The bull in musth will mate with all of the available cows in heat. After between one and thirty-four days, the male will calm down again and leave the herd. Musth, however, is not necessarily related to breeding. Females seem to prefer males in musth, but a male can breed even when he is not in musth.

### Wild Animals and Humans

Competition for land between elephants and humans has always caused problems for elephant populations. But because elephants have been an important part of the Asian economy for so many years, it became important for the people living in this part of the world to try to protect the animals. The first elephants to be used for human labor cleared trees from the woods along the Indian River 5,500 years ago. Hundreds of thousands of elephants have since been used for the same purpose in many places. As early as the sixth century B.C., Indian rulers tried to set aside protected areas for elephant herds living in the wild because elephants were essential for many jobs in India. Ironically, trade in elephants actually extended the range of elephants in Asia as working elephants escaped and became naturalized in some geographical areas.

In early times, Asian lords enjoyed hunting elephants. They also used thousands of elephants for hard labor, and in parades and battles. Later, colonial masters used elephants in the practice of the *keddah*, or the systematic capture of work elephants. A

they are much more efficient at clearing forests than are machines. Most of the elephants captured now are used for work, not for circuses.

In spite of the long colonial domination of Asia by the British and other Europeans, elephant training was always in the hands of the local populations. There are many traditional methods for training elephants, and these vary from place to place. For example, the people of Thailand use a different method than the people of Burma, and the Indians use a method that is different from the other two. For many of the masters, or *mahouts*, the elephants become part of their families. In many cases, the mahouts actually live with the elephants twenty-four hours a day. Their elephants are essential to their

large area of land was enclosed within an elephant-proof wooden fence. There was only one opening through which the elephants could enter the area. Once inside, the elephants could not exit from this opening. Several days before the roundup, a group of people would find a wild herd and drive it toward the enclosure using fire and smoke. The elephants would then be trapped inside the fence. Next, specially outfitted work elephants, called *kumkies*, were released into the group. They calmed their fellow elephants and helped separate them one by one to be trained for work by humans.

### Elephant School
The practice of keddah is still important in some places. Work elephants are much in demand in certain areas of the world, since

**Opposite:  Returning home after a day's labor.**

**Above:  What elephants enjoy most – a nice, refreshing bath.**

**Right:  An elephant at work, dragging a boat across land.**

well-being, and the trainers take excellent care of their animals. Elephants are intelligent animals and can learn an average of twenty-two commands and actions. Elephants that are especially clever can learn as many as forty commands.

Before elephants begin their day's work, they are bathed and carefully scrubbed to remove parasites from their hide. Then the work begins. The elephants fell trees and drag them to a pile where they are stacked.

The elephants' skills are most valuable in forest areas that are hard for people to reach. Elephants have a clear advantage over trucks and other mechanical vehicles in this regard. The light-footed animals don't leave much of a trail on the jungle floor and thus don't harm the other vegetation. In addition, they instinctively know the shortest way to get from the felling site back to the log pile. Elephants work for a maximum of seven hours a day with several rest periods or breaks, and then they are free to eat in the woods for the rest of the time.

*Above, right:  Parade elephants are always bull elephants with tusks.*

*Above, center:  A parade of war elephants carved into an Indian temple.*

*Right:  An Indian lord had a huge fountain decorated with elephant statues built in his garden.*

*Right: In this painting, an Indian war elephant panics on a bridge and attacks the elephant in front of him. The artwork comes from India and is about four hundred years old.*

# Hope for Survival

During the last few years, life has become very difficult for elephants, especially the African elephants. Bands of poachers equipped with the most up-to-date weapons have been killing these animals in large

*Above: In Zaire, Africa, home to this wild elephant, three-quarters of the elephant population was killed during the 1980s.*

numbers. In earlier times, elephants lived such a long time that their tusks sometimes grew to weigh 220 pounds (100 kg). But now, many animals live only long enough for their tusks to weigh a mere 11 to 22 pounds (5 to 10 kg). In many countries, national park authorities are powerless to do anything to prevent the excessive hunting of elephants. They simply do not have as many weapons as the poachers.

One main reason for the massacre of elephants is clear. Their ivory tusks are extremely valuable. Traders will pay top dollar for ivory, especially in the Far East. Hong Kong, for example, imported the tusks of between 25,000 and 30,000 elephants in 1975 alone. Japan is also a major consumer of elephant ivory. To complicate this problem, some African countries that have laws protecting and regulating the elephant population feel the ban on ivory is unfair and has cost them much needed revenue.

A second major reason for the disappearance of the elephants is the fact that their natural habitats are shrinking. The human populations of Africa and southern Asia are growing rapidly. People need land for crops and are pushing back farther and farther into the elephants' domain. Because of this, the animals aren't able either to migrate or to travel as far for food, and they are forced to eat too many of the plants growing in their own reserves. The trees suffer the greatest damage. In Asia and India, elephants have suffered the greatest losses of habitat. Hungry and desperate, they sometimes break into farmland to find food and are then either captured or killed.

The end result of these factors is tragic. In Africa alone, more than half of the elephant population has been lost in the last ten years. There are now only about 600,000 left. In all of Asia, there are only about 40,000 wild elephants left.

A glimmer of hope for the wild elephants of the world has been made possible by the outpouring of concern by people everywhere. Hopefully, their actions will allow elephants to remain healthy, vital members of the world's animal population.

# *APPENDIX*
# *TO*
# *ANIMAL FAMILIES*

## ELEPHANTS

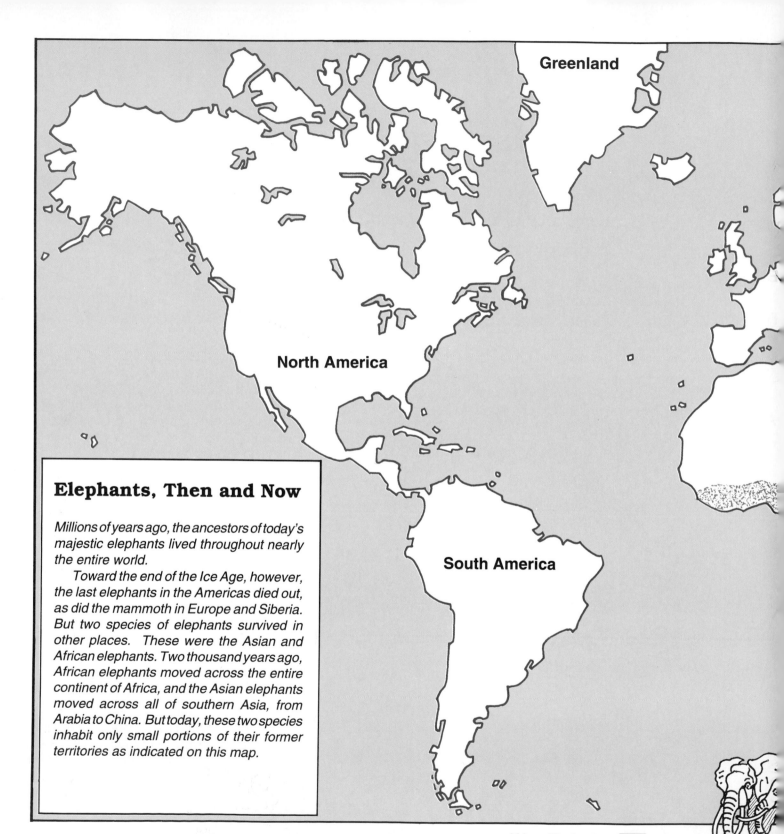

**Greenland**

**North America**

**South America**

## Elephants, Then and Now

*Millions of years ago, the ancestors of today's majestic elephants lived throughout nearly the entire world.*

*Toward the end of the Ice Age, however, the last elephants in the Americas died out, as did the mammoth in Europe and Siberia. But two species of elephants survived in other places. These were the Asian and African elephants. Two thousand years ago, African elephants moved across the entire continent of Africa, and the Asian elephants moved across all of southern Asia, from Arabia to China. But today, these two species inhabit only small portions of their former territories as indicated on this map.*

*African Elephants*

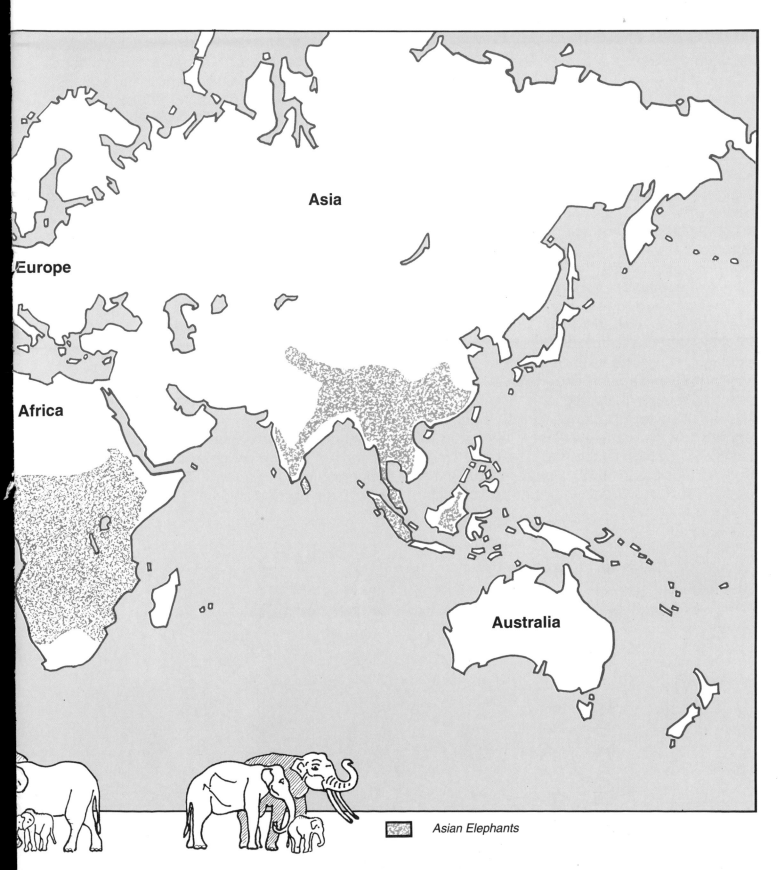

Europe

Asia

Africa

Australia

Asian Elephants

43

# ABOUT THESE BOOKS

Although this series is called "Animal Families," these books aren't just about fathers, mothers, and young. They also discuss the scientific definition of *family,* which is a division of biological classification and includes many animals.

Biological classification is a method that scientists use to identify and organize living things. Using this system, scientists place animals and plants into larger groups that share similar characteristics. Characteristics are physical features, natural habits, ancestral backgrounds, or any other qualities that make one organism either like or different from another.

The method used today for biological classification was introduced in 1753 by a Swedish botanist-naturalist named Carolus Linnaeus. Although many scientists tried to find ways to classify the world's plants and animals, Linnaeus's system seemed to be the only useful choice. Charles Darwin, a famous British naturalist, referred to Linnaeus's system in his theory of evolution, which was published in his book *On the Origin of Species* in 1859. Linnaeus's system of classification, shown below, includes seven major categories, or groups. These are: kingdom, phylum, class, order, family, genus, and species.

An easy way to remember the divisions and their order is to memorize this sentence: "Ken Put Cake On Frank's Good Shirt." The first letter of each word in this sentence gives you the first letter of a division. (The *K* in *Ken*, for example, stands for *kingdom*.) The order of the words in this sentence suggests the order of the divisions from largest to smallest. The kingdom is the largest of these divisions; the species is the smallest. The larger the division, the more types of animals or plants it contains. For example, the animal kingdom, called Animalia, contains everything from worms to whales. Smaller divisions, such as the family, have fewer members that share more characteristics. For example, members of the bear family, Ursidae, include the polar bear, the brown bear, and many others.

In the following chart, the lion species is followed through all seven categories. As the categories expand to include more and more members, remember that only a few examples are pictured here. Each division has many more members.

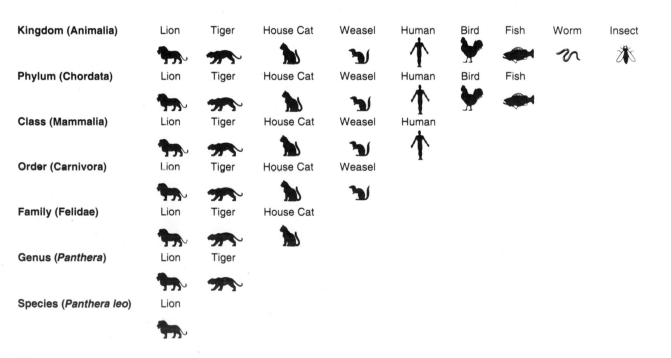

| | Lion | Tiger | House Cat | Weasel | Human | Bird | Fish | Worm | Insect |
|---|---|---|---|---|---|---|---|---|---|
| **Kingdom (Animalia)** | Lion | Tiger | House Cat | Weasel | Human | Bird | Fish | Worm | Insect |
| **Phylum (Chordata)** | Lion | Tiger | House Cat | Weasel | Human | Bird | Fish | | |
| **Class (Mammalia)** | Lion | Tiger | House Cat | Weasel | Human | | | | |
| **Order (Carnivora)** | Lion | Tiger | House Cat | Weasel | | | | | |
| **Family (Felidae)** | Lion | Tiger | House Cat | | | | | | |
| **Genus (*Panthera*)** | Lion | Tiger | | | | | | | |
| **Species (*Panthera leo*)** | Lion | | | | | | | | |

# SCIENTIFIC NAMES OF THE ANIMALS IN THIS BOOK

Animals have different names in every language. For this reason, researchers the world over use the same scientific names, which usually stem from ancient Greek or Latin. Most animals are classified by two names. One is the genus name; the other is the name of the species to which they belong. Additional names indicate further subgroupings. The scientific names for the animals included in *Elephants* are:

African elephant ...................................... *Loxodonta africana*
Asian elephant .......................................... *Elephas maximus*

# GLOSSARY

**breed**
To produce offspring.

**bulls**
Male elephants. Bulls leave their mother's herd as soon as they reach puberty and join together in groups.

**class**
The third of seven divisions in the biological classification system proposed by Swedish botanist-naturalist Carolus Linnaeus. The class is the main subdivision of the phylum. Elephants belong to the class Mammalia. Animals in this class, which includes humans, share certain features: they have skin covered with hair, they give birth to live young, and they nourish the young with milk from mammary glands.

**cow**
A female elephant. Elephant family groups are usually led by an experienced cow, called a matriarch.

**docile**
Easy to teach or manage. Although they are huge and powerful animals, elephants are basically docile and peaceful creatures and can be trained very easily.

**extinct**
No longer existing; completely destroyed or killed off. Many beautiful and exotic plant and animal species that once existed on Earth are now extinct.

**family**
The fifth of seven divisions in the biological classification system proposed by Swedish botanist-naturalist Carolus Linnaeus. Elephants belong to the family Elephantidae.

**genus** (plural: **genera**)
The sixth division in the biological classification system proposed by Swedish botanist-naturalist Carolus Linnaeus. A genus is the main subdivision of a family and includes one or more species.

**gestation period**
The number of days from actual conception to the birth of an animal. Gestation periods vary greatly for different types of animals. The gestation period for an elephant is usually twenty-two months. Elephant babies, or calves, weigh about 220 pounds (100 kg) at birth.

**habitat**
The natural living area or environment in which an animal usually lives.

**incisor**
A sharp tooth for cutting. The upper incisors of the elephant evolved into tusks.

**infrasonic**
Sound waves elephants use to communicate with each other that are inaudible to humans.

**ivory**
The hard white substance from the tusk of an elephant. The sale of ivory is forbidden in many countries in an effort to protect the elephant.

**kingdom**
The first of seven divisions in the biological classification system proposed by Swedish botanist-naturalist Carolus Linnaeus. Animals, including humans, belong to the kingdom Animalia. It is one of five kingdoms.

**ligature**
Something that ties or binds. The web of elastic ligature in an elephant's feet cushions its step.

**mammoth**
An extinct, hairy relative of the elephant. Mammoths were well-adapted to the cold climate in which they lived because of their thick coat of hair.

**mastodon**
A giant, extinct animal that originated in Africa about twenty million years ago. Tusks grew from upper and lower jaws in the mastodon.

**migration**
The movement of animals or people from one place to another. Occasionally during great migrations, related herds of animals join together and form giant herds of hundreds of animals.

**molar**
A large grinding tooth. An elephant's molar is about the size of a brick. Although an elephant is equipped with six, only one is used at a time.

**musth**
A regular period of unpredictable, aggressive behavior during which a black, oily, strong-smelling secretion is produced by the male elephant's temple, or temporal, glands. A bull elephant in musth is ready to mate and is extremely aggressive.

**nurse**
To drink milk from a mother's mammary glands. Young mammals receive nourishment in this manner.

**order**
The fourth of seven divisions in the biological classification system proposed by the Swedish botanist-naturalist Carolus Linnaeus. The order is the main subdivision of the class and contains many different families. Elephants belong to the order Proboscidea.

**phylum** (plural: **phyla**)
The second of seven divisions in the biological classification system proposed by the Swedish botanist-naturalist Carolus Linnaeus. A phylum is one of the main divisions of a kingdom.

**poacher**
A person who hunts illegally.

**predecessor**
A forerunner. The forerunners of elephants evolved about fifty million years ago.

**prehistoric times**
The period before history was recorded.

**prototype**
An original model. A museum model of a mammoth skeleton had the tusks pointing in the wrong direction, which led to many museums reconstructing the mammoth skeletons in error.

**savanna**
A treeless plain.

**species**
The last of seven divisions in the biological classification system proposed by Swedish botanist-naturalist Carolus Linnaeus. The species is the main subdivision of the genus. It may include further subgroups of its own, called subspecies. At the level of species, members share many features and are capable of breeding with one another.

**submerged**
Placed or plunged under the surface. Elephants can breathe through their trunks even if the rest of their bodies are completely under water.

**tusk**
A long, protruding tooth. An elephant's tusks, which are made of ivory, can be as long as 3 feet (1 m). Elephants use their tusks to dig holes in the earth, to mine for salt, to peel bark off of trees, to scare away rivals, and to make an impression on the opposite sex.

# MORE BOOKS ABOUT ELEPHANTS

*Elephant.* Mary Hoffman (Raintree Steck-Vaughn)
*Elephant.* Sarah Blakeman (Troll Associates)
*Elephant in the Bush.* Ian Redmond (Gareth Stevens)
*Elephant Memories: 13 Years in the Life of an Elephant Family.* Cynthia Moss (Morrow)
*Elephants.* Miriam Schlein (Atheneum)
*Elephants.* Wildlife Education, Ltd. (Wildlife Education)
*Elephants of Africa.* Paul Bosman and Anthony Hall-Martini (Safari Press)

# PLACES TO WRITE

The following are some of the many organizations that exist to educate people about animals, promote the protection of animals, and encourage the conservation of their environments. Write to these organizations for more information about elephants, other animals, or animal concerns of interest to you. When you write, include your name, address, and age, and tell them clearly what you want to know. Don't forget to enclose a stamped, self-addressed envelope for a reply.

East African Wildlife Society
P.O. Box 20110
Nairobi, Kenya

Save African Endangered Wildlife
 Foundation
230 Park Avenue, Suite 2711
New York, NY 10017

International Union for Conservation
 of Nature and Natural Resources
 (IUCN)
World Conservation Center
Avenue du Mont Blanc
CH-1196 Gland, Switzerland

TRAFFIC (USA)
1250 24th Street, N.W.
Washington, D.C. 20037

Wildlife Conservation International
185th Street & Southern Boulevard
Bronx, NY 10460

# THINGS TO DO

These projects are designed to help you have fun with what you've learned about elephants. You can do them alone, in small groups, or as a class project.

1. Visit the zoo nearest your home or in another city if you are going on a trip or vacation. See if you can tell the African elephants from the Asian elephants by looking at the end of their trunks. See if you can sense the infrasonic communication among the elephants.

2. Visit your local museum to view the prehistoric display. If there is a mammoth or a mastodon, discuss their similarities and differences with today's elephants.

3. Sculpt an Asian and/or African elephant to scale based on the descriptions in the book. Use store-bought modeling clay, or make your own by mixing 2 cups (.48 l) table salt with 2/3 cup (.16 l) warm water. Cook over low heat, stirring constantly for three to four minutes. Have an adult help you when using the stove. Remove from heat. Mix 1 cup (.24 l) of cornstarch and 1/2 cup (.12 l) of cold water and add all to your cooked water/salt mixture. Stir quickly. Sculpt into an elephant, and let dry. Once dry, your sculpture can be painted with poster paints.

# INDEX